Let's Meet
Booker T. Washington

"The best way to lift one's self up is to help some one else."
—Booker T. Washington

J
B
Washington

Helen Frost

CHELSEA CLUBHOUSE

An Imprint of Chelsea House Publishers

A Haights Cross Communications Company

Philadelphia

Chelsea Clubhouse books are published by Chelsea House Publishers, a subsidiary of Haights Cross Communications.

A Haights Cross Communications Company

The Chelsea House World Wide Web address is www.chelseahouse.com

Printed and bound in the United States of America.

9 8 7 6 5 4 3 2 1

Library of Congress Cataloging-in-Publication Data
Frost, Helen, 1949–
    Let's meet Booker T. Washington / Helen Frost.
        p. cm. — (Let's meet biographies)
Summary: Simple text and photographs introduce the life of Booker T. Washington, including his childhood, education, founding of Tuskegee Institute, and public speaking.
Includes bibliographical references and index.
ISBN 0-7910-7318-1
1. Washington, Booker T., 1856–1915—Juvenile literature. 2. African Americans—
Biography—Juvenile literature. 3. Educators—United States—Biography—Juvenile literature.
[1. Washington, Booker T., 1856–1915. 2. Educators. 3. African Americans—Biography.]
I. Title. II. Series.
E185.97.W4F76 2004
370'.92—dc21   2003004745

Editorial Credits

Lois Wallentine, editor; Takeshi Takahashi, designer; Mary Englar, photo researcher; Jennifer Krassy Peiler, layout

Content Reviewer

Cynthia B. Wilson, Program Director, Tuskegee University Archives and Museums, Tuskegee, Ala.

Photo Credits

©CORBIS: cover; AP/Wide World: title page; North Wind Picture Archives: 4, 8, 19, 20; Virginia State Library and Archives: 5; ©Bettmann/CORBIS: 6, 12, 21; Tuskegee University Archives: 7, 11, 13, 15, 16, 17 (top and bottom), 22, 23, 24, 26, 27, 29; Hampton University Archives, 9, 10, 25; Library of Congress: 14 (top and bottom); Schomburg Center for Research in Black Culture, New York Public Library, Astor, Lenox and Tilden Foundations: 18.

Table of Contents

Wanting to Learn

Booker T. Washington was born into **slavery**. His mother, Jane, was a cook on her master's farm. He never knew his father. As a boy, he was called just "Booker." He didn't have a last name.

Booker never knew the exact date of his birth. Today, people believe it was April 5, 1856.

Booker lived in this slave cabin with his mother; his brother, John; and his sister, Amanda. The cabin was on a farm near Hales Ford, Virginia.

Booker said that being able to go to a school like this one "would be about the same as getting into **paradise**."

When he was a child, Booker never had time to play. He carried water to slaves working in the fields. He worked in the master's house. He carried schoolbooks for his master's children.

Booker wanted to learn to read. But slaves were not allowed to go to school.

In the salt furnace, Booker packed salt into barrels marked with the number 18. It was the first number Booker learned to read.

When Booker was 9 years old, the **Civil War** ended. All slaves became free. Booker's family traveled to Malden, West Virginia, to join his stepfather.

A school for black children opened in a nearby town. Booker wanted to go to school, but his family needed money. Booker went to work in a **salt furnace** and later in a **coal mine**.

Booker started taking lessons from the teacher at night. But he kept asking to go to the day school. Finally, his stepfather agreed. But Booker had to work for five hours before school and two hours after school.

Booker's Name

On the first day of school, Booker realized he needed a last name. He called himself "Booker Washington." Washington was his stepfather's first name. Later he found out his mother had named him "Booker Taliaferro" (say ta-luh-FER-oh). He started signing his name as "Booker T. Washington."

Booker T. Washington

At age 16, Booker decided to go to a school for black students called Hampton Institute. It was about 500 miles (805 kilometers) away. Booker took a train and then a **stagecoach** until his money ran out. Then he walked and asked for rides when he could.

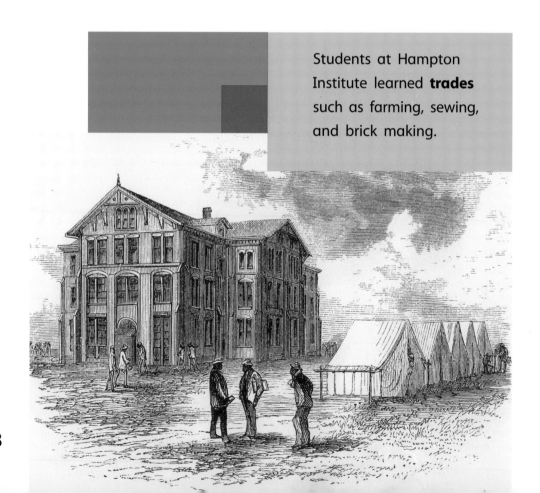

Students at Hampton Institute learned **trades** such as farming, sewing, and brick making.

Miss Mackie gave Booker a job cleaning rooms at the school. He earned money to pay for his room and food.

Booker was hungry and dirty when he arrived at Hampton. The head teacher, Mary Mackie, was not sure she should let him become a student. She asked Booker to clean a classroom. He cleaned the room so well that Miss Mackie said, "I guess you will do to enter this **institution**."

Building a School

Booker studied at Hampton Institute for three years. In 1875, he **graduated** with honors. He was trained to be a teacher.

Booker went back to Malden to teach school. He taught children during the day and adults at night.

Booker and his classmates and teachers pose for a graduation photo.

Booker

In 1879, Booker returned to Hampton Institute as a teacher. He taught the school's first group of American Indian students.

In 1881, Booker was chosen to start a school in Tuskegee, Alabama. The school would train black students to be teachers.

Booker was 25 years old when he started Tuskegee State Normal School. The school would later become known as Tuskegee Institute.

The plantation Booker bought had a few old buildings that could be fixed up for the school's use.

Booker had to find buildings for the new school. He first held classes in an old church. He had 30 students.

Every month, new students arrived. The school soon needed more space. Booker borrowed money to buy an old **plantation**. He and the students fixed up the buildings. They used these spaces for classrooms and housing.

The students built their own beds and made mattresses. They planted a garden for food. They learned to make bricks and build buildings.

Some students didn't like all the work. But Booker worked along with them and said, "Labor is **dignified** and beautiful." Soon the students began to take pride in hard work.

Students used the bricks they made for new buildings. Here, students work on a classroom building. It was finished in 1909.

Students learn to set type to print newspapers.

As the school grew, Booker added classes. He wanted to prepare students for many types of jobs. Students learned skills in farming, carpentry, printing, dress making, and many other trades.

Students show the steps to making a mattress.

Olivia Davidson started teaching at the school in 1881. She later became Booker's second wife.

Olivia Davidson was one of the school's first teachers. She also helped Booker raise money for the school. Booker and Olivia traveled to visit people who gave **donations**. The money paid for the land and new school buildings.

George Washington Carver was best known for studying peanuts. He made ink, soap, face powder, and many other products from peanuts.

Booker hired more staff members as the school grew. One was a scientist and teacher named George Washington Carver. He led farming classes and ran the school's farms. He showed people how to produce more food from their crops.

Booker was married three times. He married Fannie Smith in 1882. They had a daughter, Portia. Fannie died in 1884 after a fall.

Booker married Olivia Davidson in 1885. They had two sons named Booker Jr. (called "Baker") and Ernest Davidson (called "Dave"). Olivia died in 1889 from an illness.

Booker married his third wife, Margaret Murray, in 1893. They later adopted Margaret's niece, Laura Murray.

Fannie

From left to right: Dave, Baker, Margaret, Booker, Portia

Speaking about Respect

Booker often gave speeches about his ideas on education. Some people thought students should learn only from books. But Booker wanted to be sure his students would find jobs. He said students should also learn from working. He believed everyone would respect skill and hard work.

Booker

Booker stands on a platform to speak to this large crowd in Iowa.

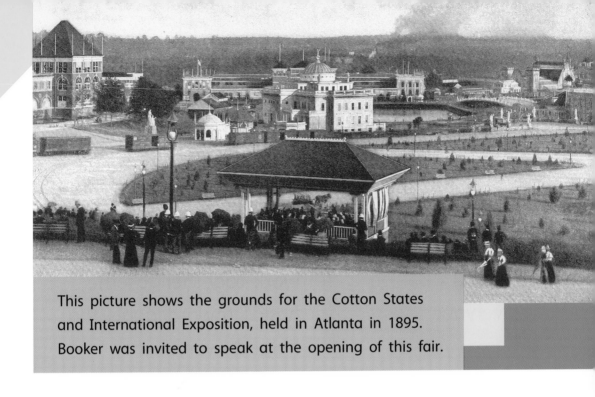

This picture shows the grounds for the Cotton States and International Exposition, held in Atlanta in 1895. Booker was invited to speak at the opening of this fair.

On September 18, 1895, Booker spoke at an important **exposition** in Atlanta, Georgia. Some people in the large audience had once been slaves. Some had been slave owners. Some had fought to end slavery.

Booker wanted to help people understand each other. He told the audience that black people and white people shared a country. They should work together and respect each other.

Booker did not **demand** equal rights for everyone. He said in their personal lives, blacks and whites could be "as separate as the fingers." But they could work together "as the hand" toward goals that helped everyone.

The audience cheered for Booker. The governor of Georgia shook his hand.

At the fair, one building held displays of goods and services offered by black people. In this painting, President Grover Cleveland is shown visiting the building.

Booker's ideas became part of an important **debate** about rights and education. Some people disagreed with Booker. They said blacks and whites should always be treated equally.

But Booker believed blacks had to first learn skills and trades. He wanted blacks to buy their own land and run their own businesses. Then blacks would earn respect and fair treatment.

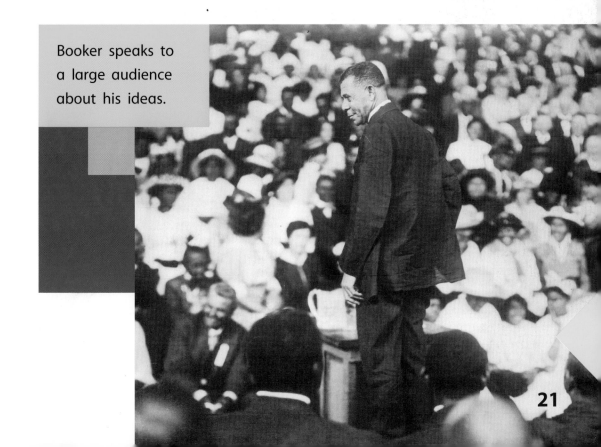

Booker speaks to a large audience about his ideas.

Remembering Booker

Booker became a well-known speaker. He met three presidents of the United States and the queen of England. He gave speeches and talked to people about his school. Many people gave money for new buildings and **scholarships**.

President Theodore Roosevelt stands next to Booker to watch a parade on the school grounds. The president visited Tuskegee Institute on the school's 25th anniversary.

Booker and his two sons go for a ride around the school grounds.

Booker always made sure the school was running smoothly. He received daily updates when he was traveling. When he was home, he often rode his horse around the school grounds. He paid attention to what teachers and students were doing.

In 1896, leaders at Harvard University gave Booker an **honorary degree**. It was the first time the university had given this award to a black person. In 1901, Booker also received an honorary degree from Yale University.

Booker received honors from both Harvard and Yale Universities.

Booker's book *Up from Slavery* tells about his childhood as a slave, his longing to go to school, and his work for Tuskegee Institute.

UP FROM SLAVERY

AN AUTOBIOGRAPHY

By BOOKER T. WASHINGTON

Author of "The Future of the American Negro."

A. L. BURT COMPANY, Publishers
NEW YORK

Booker wrote the story of his life. The book was called *Up from Slavery*. It was published in 1901 and has stayed in print for more than 100 years. Booker also wrote many articles on his experiences and beliefs about education.

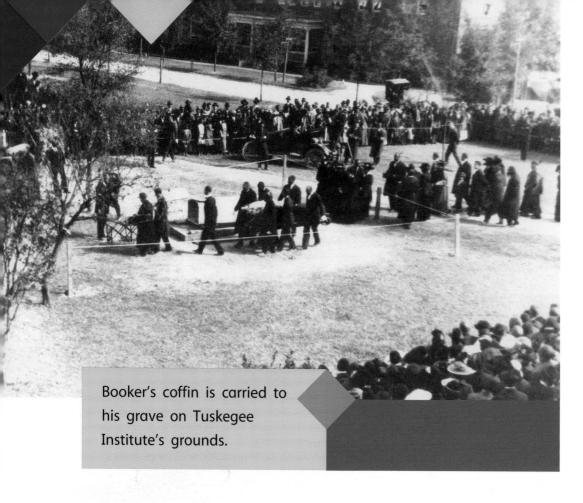

Booker's coffin is carried to his grave on Tuskegee Institute's grounds.

In November 1915, Booker became very ill while on a trip to New York. He asked the doctors to send him home. Booker and his wife took a train back to Tuskegee. He died at his home on November 14, 1915. He was 59 years old.

Tuskegee Institute is now called Tuskegee University. Students from many backgrounds go to school there. People remember Booker T. Washington as the school's **founder** and as a great leader.

This monument to Booker was built in 1922 on the Tuskegee school grounds. The monument honors Booker for helping others see the importance of education.

Important Dates in Booker's Life

1856 Booker T. Washington is born in Hales Ford, Virginia.

1865 The Civil War ends; many slaves become free; Booker moves with his family to Malden, West Virginia.

Age 16 **1872** Booker travels to Hampton, Virginia; he starts school at Hampton Institute.

1875 Booker graduates from Hampton Institute; he returns to Malden to teach at a nearby school.

1879 Booker returns to Hampton Institute as a teacher.

Age 25 **1881** Booker opens a school in Tuskegee, Alabama.

1882 Booker marries Fannie Smith.

1883 Booker's daughter, Portia, is born.

1884 Fannie (Smith) Washington dies.

1885 Booker marries Olivia Davidson; son Baker is born.

1889 Booker's son Dave is born; Olivia (Davidson) Washington dies.

1892 Booker marries Margaret Murray; later he adopts her niece, Laura Murray.

Age 39 **1895** Booker gives an important speech in Atlanta, Georgia, on September 18.

1896 Booker receives an honorary degree from Harvard University.

1901 Booker publishes his book, *Up from Slavery*; he receives an honorary degree from Yale University.

Age 59 **1915** Booker dies at his home on the Tuskegee Institute grounds on November 14.

More about Tuskegee University

Today there are 106 colleges and universities in the United States that started as schools for black students. They are known as Historically Black Colleges and Universities. That name is sometimes shortened to HBCU. Tuskegee Institute—which was renamed Tuskegee University in 1985—is an HBCU.

Tuskegee University's front gates feature the school's seal with an image of Booker T. Washington.

Tuskegee University is one of only a few HBCUs to be started, owned, and operated by black people. Many other HBCUs were started in the 1800s by state governments or by white people who wanted to help runaway slaves and free blacks. When town leaders in Tuskegee, Alabama, decided to open a school for blacks, they asked the principal at Hampton Institute to recommend a white person to be the new school's leader. The principal replied, "The only man I can suggest is one Mr. Booker T. Washington… I know of no white man who would do better." Booker accepted the challenge. He hired black teachers and staff, and he made sure the school—not the state—owned the land and buildings.

During his 34 years as the school's president, Booker saw the number of students grow from 30 to about 3,000. He watched the students put up about 50 new buildings and learn skills in a wide variety of trades.

Today Tuskegee University continues to grow. The campus has 75 major buildings. It offers degrees in more than 50 programs including veterinary science, engineering, nursing, business, architecture, and many more. In its long history, tens of thousands of students have attended the school that Booker started in order to "lift up" others.

Glossary

Civil War—the U.S. war between the northern and the southern states that lasted from 1861 to 1865

coal mine—an underground tunnel where miners dig coal to use as fuel

debate—a discussion between people with different ideas

demand—to claim something or ask firmly for something

dignified—honorable or noble

donations—gifts of money; many people gave money to Tuskegee Institute to build new buildings, buy books and supplies, and support students.

exposition—a large fair featuring displays of products

founder—a person who sets up or starts something, such as a school

graduated—completed the last year in a school

honorary degree—a title or degree given by a college or university to show respect for someone; the person does not have to take classes in order to receive the degree.

institution—an organization in which people work together; schools were sometimes called institutions.

paradise—a place that is beautiful and makes people feel happy

plantation—a large farm; in southern states, many plantations grew crops such as cotton.

salt furnace—a place where salt water is piped into furnaces and boiled dry; the salt that is left at the end is packed into barrels; Booker's job was to shovel salt into barrels.

scholarship—a grant or prize that pays for a student to go to a school or college

slavery—the practice of forcing people to work without pay

stagecoach—a type of wagon that carried people and was pulled by horses

trades—jobs that involve working with the hands or with machines

To Learn More

▶ **Read these books:**

Amper, Thomas. *Booker T. Washington*. Minneapolis: Carolrhoda Books, 1998.

Bradby, Marie. *More Than Anything Else*. New York: Orchard Books, 1995.

Schaefer, Lola M. *Booker T. Washington*. First Biographies. Mankato, Minn.: Pebble Books, 2003.

▶ **Look up these Web sites:**

African-American Odyssey—The Booker T. Washington Era

memory.loc.gov/ammem/aaohtml/exhibit/aopart6.html
  Learn more facts about the times in which Booker lived.

Booker T. Washington National Monument

www.nps.gov/bowa/
  See the cabin where Booker was born, which is now a National Monument. Click on the "in depth" button for more information.

Legends of Tuskegee

www.cr.nps.gov/museum/exhibits/tuskegee/index.htm
  View many photos and read more about Booker's life.

Tuskegee University

www.tuskegee.edu
  Click on the words "History & Archives" to go to a page about the university's history. The "Legacy of Leadership" link will lead you to more information about Booker's life.

▶ **Key Internet search terms:**

Booker T. Washington, Tuskegee University, slavery

Index

Dec. 2003